T0165609

My Life
Journey

John Kim, Ph.D., P.E.

WESTBOW
PRESS®
A DIVISION OF THOMAS NELSON
& ZONDERVAN

WestBow Press books may be ordered through booksellers or by contacting:

WestBow Press
A Division of Thomas Nelson & Zondervan
1663 Liberty Drive
Bloomington, IN 47403
www.westbowpress.com
1 (866) 928-1240

Because of the dynamic nature of the Internet, any web addresses or
links contained in this book may have changed since publication and
may no longer be valid. The views expressed in this work are solely those
of the author and do not necessarily reflect the views of the publisher,
and the publisher hereby disclaims any responsibility for them.

Any people depicted in stock imagery provided by Thinkstock are models,
and such images are being used for illustrative purposes only.
Certain stock imagery © Thinkstock.

ISBN: 978-1-4908-1560-2 (sc)
ISBN: 978-1-4908-1561-9 (e)

Library of Congress Control Number: 2013921016

Print information available on the last page.

WestBow Press rev. date: 06/15/2020

Contents

Preface

I always wished I had known more about my early childhood—those days too young to remember—as well as about my parents and how they grew up and how they met. As I grow old and often think about my mortality, I regret that I did not ask my mom about these things when she was alive. This is why I decided to write this story about me and the events that have touched my life.

I shared this manuscript with one of my friends for his review for its worthiness. He suggested that I publish it, saying that many would enjoy reading my life story. Encouraged by this, but with some reservations, I decided to publish it. I hope my story resonates with folks, particularly immigrants and foreign students who took a similar path and endured struggles similar to mine. Many who came to America for whatever reason may concur with me that living in an adopted land is analogous to living in an apartment. You long for a place you can call a home, but you come to a realization that there is not such a place.

CHAPTER 1

Childhood

Although I lived in Korea for all of my childhood, I was born in Jiujiang, China, during World War II. My family moved to China before the war; my father was running a sugar import business there. My mom was pregnant with me. The war was turning in favor of the Allies, and the Japanese had begun to retreat from some parts of China.

My family lived in a large, two-story house. I was due any day, and my mom felt it was safer to have a baby in the shelter rather than in her house. Our shelter was nothing more than a large, horizontal, underground hole with a small entrance. It looked like plain, flat ground when viewed from a warplane so it would be an unlikely bombing target.

So the whole family moved to the shelter. And our house—one of the largest buildings in our neighborhood—was bombed by a US warplane. The pilot might have misjudged it for something other than a home. Mom told me that I saved the whole family; I was a miracle baby. With no house to live in and increasing violence, my family decided to go back home. It was a long, horrifying five-day journey by train to Korea.

My mom witnessed many killings and rapes during the trip back to Korea. She said that the whole region was so chaotic; there was no way to know who controlled each town. As the train passed through towns in China on the way to Korea, one town could still be under the retreating Japanese force, while the next town could be under the Chinese rebels. And in yet another town, it was unclear who was in charge.

"I had to shave my head to look like a man to avoid being dragged out of the train and getting raped—and who knows what afterward," Mom said. "We would have all been killed had we stayed there a few more weeks." The Chinese considered us Japanese. "Had our house not been bombed, we probably would have stayed there longer," Mom told me. "By then, we would have no means to come back home." Train services were suspended shortly after we left due to the increased violence. So America saved us by bombing our house. What irony!

My earliest memory goes back to the time when I was probably four or five years old and visiting my grandfather's house. He was a Chinese medical doctor. I remember little about him, Grandma, or his house. All I remember is that his house was covered with many, many bags of dried weeds and medicinal twigs. The ceiling was completely covered with dangling bags. Tall chests with many drawers blocked all four walls, except the areas where the doors were. As soon as I got there, I ran straight to those chests. I knew exactly which chest and which two drawers to open among hundreds of drawers for cinnamon and licorice root. I chewed and chewed them until they did not taste so good. Then I spat them out and put another batch of fresh bark in my mouth.

I also remember my visit to my other grandfather on my mom's side. He was a doctor, one of the few Western doctors in the country back then. At his house I ate beef cubes and garlic cloves preserved in soy sauce. Those were so tasty—a rare treat I could not find in my house. He lived in a regular-looking, thatched house. From the outside, you would not know it was a clinic. His house had a wooden box as big as a refrigerator. I often wondered who was inside, talking all the time. No other house in our town had a radio back then.

I remember the first day of the Korean War. It was an early morning and was drizzling outside. We walked a very long walk; it seemed we had walked all day. When I asked my mom about that long walk, she said we walked to a temple in the mountain, not too far from our house. She added, "A temple in the mountain was a safe place for our family to hide." So, I began to think that there could be a wide gap between my childhood memories and the actual incidents.

I remember some of the Korean War, but most of it I learned from my mom. I was six or seven and had just started first grade. I was so excited when I received the brand-new textbooks. Back then, the school started early in spring. We lived in a small town on an island west of Seoul, called Kangwha-Do, just below the DMZ. The DMZ is a demilitarized strip of land running across Korea between North and South Korea. North Korea had just invaded South Korea. So we had no time to prepare to move very far.

At that time, my father was working for the town. The North Korean soldiers were instructed to kill any government or town officials first, before anybody else. My father was in hiding, going from place to place. Thank heaven, they were not able to find him.

Several months into the war, I remember seeing my mom crying for a long time. I thought that I had done something bad and I wanted to say to her "I am sorry", but I later found out that one of my older brothers was killed by a US warplane. The United States imposed a curfew day and night to thwart enemy movements. No one was allowed to be seen in the street. My brother, who was ten or eleven, had been on his way to the market to buy rice. My mom had my three-year-old brother and six-month-old sister to nourish.

Townspeople still moved around in stealth, evading the overhead warplanes. I loved to look up at the skies to see airplanes flying high above, wondering if I would ever have a chance to fly on an airplane before I died. It is an irony that warplanes, which represent fear and

3

destruction to many, can be the source of fascination and dreams for a child.

Most of the North Korean soldiers were young boys, about fourteen or fifteen years old. My mom asked these kid soldiers, "Why are you here?" They just shrugged timidly. Mom also told me that we had moved so many times during the war that she had to think hard to remember all the places where we had stayed.

My memories about the war and what I did during the war are blurry and patchy. However, I remember my mom taking me to school one winter day and enrolling me in a second or third grade. I am not sure now if the war was over. It was the first time I had stepped in the classroom since the war began. Although I was eight or nine, I did not know how to read, let alone add and subtract.

I had been in first grade for only three months when the war broke out. In those days in Korea, your age dictated what grade you needed to be in. My class consisted of one female teacher and nearly one hundred students. One teacher for so many students would be shocking by today's standard. And you may wonder how one teacher could deal with so many students in the class. Believe me, the entire class was quiet as a mouse.

Back then, teachers in Korea were highly respected, even more than doctors. They were given all the authority to punish rowdy students. Corporal punishments were handed out routinely. I received more punishments than any of the other students, mostly in the form of physical labor. Every school day, I, along with a few not-so-bright students, had to stay after class. Our job was mopping the floor and tidying up the classroom after school. There were no hired janitors to do this job. Students who received low test scores on a particular day were given the cleaning assignment. I did more than poorly on my tests. Here is how bad I was: When the assignment was to find the opposite word, I would write the opposite—for example, *tall* was *llat*.

My mom was a devoted Christian, so we attended church every Sunday. The church was on a hilltop overlooking the harbor, the ocean, and the whole city. The hill was covered with mostly acacia trees. I still remember the sweet fragrance of acacia flowers wafting through the open church windows as a gentle breeze passed by. I sat next to my mom, half sleeping and half awake during a long sermon. I was probably eleven or twelve and was very naïve for that age. During the offering prayers, I often heard that money would be used for God's work. "How will money fly up to God?" I wondered. One Sunday, I found out the money was not used by God but spent down here. I felt betrayed and lost my desire to go to church. Since then, I've gone to church from time to time, mainly to please my mom.

CHAPTER 2

Early Adulthood

When I graduated from high school, I applied for the Korean Air Force Academy. My two brothers were in college, and I knew my parents could not support three college tuitions. To my surprise, I was accepted. Those days, being an air force cadet was something to brag about. However, my elation did not last long, as I was informed that I did not pass the physical. That was when I found out I had hypertension. I also found out I'd had tuberculosis when I was very young, but had completely recovered—with a calcified lung to prove it. I heard my mom saying that when I was an infant, I was so bony and feeble from being ill that she did not think I would make it; she had pretty much given up on me. So I was a miracle baby in more ways than one, according to her.

After finishing my high school, I had a job at a US military base in Incheon, where my father worked. It was a large base, and he was working in a different area, so I rarely saw him there. A year later, I enrolled in Inha Institute of Technology and took night classes. I received the top score on the entrance exam and was exempted from tuition for a year. I then quit my job and switched to day classes. I was doing well, earning the highest GPA in my chemical engineering department. I was awarded a scholarship from the government, so I didn't have to pay tuition for my entire college education, provided I maintained good grades.

As soon as I became a senior, I was recruited by Lucky Company (predecessor of LG Electronics). With a job already secured, I did not have a strong desire to study, but I wanted to graduate with the highest honor in my department. I had received the top honor in my class in the previous years and did not want to relinquish it. So I struggled.

During my senior year, I also received an invitation to study in the environmental engineering and science department at the University of Alaska as a research assistant. This was a relatively new field, even in the United States. There was no university in Korea that taught it. So I was excited and yet unsure of myself in this new field.

Those days, only a handful of Koreans were allowed to go overseas each year. I had to pass the *yoohak* (study abroad) exams, which included Korean history and English. My problem was not passing the exams, although I failed Korean history once, but my conscription status. The government only allowed those who had finished their mandatory military service or had been exempt from military duty (known as *byungjong*) due to the medical reasons to leave the country. I had received the byungjong status previously, due to my hypertension.

But the military government decided to invalidate all the byungjong statuses given by the previous nonmilitary government. The new government believed that most byungjong men had gotten that status illegitimately by bribing officials. So the government prevented all byungjong men from leaving the country.

I had already quit my new job at Lucky Company in preparation to go to the United States. I still remember the agony on my boss's face when I told him I needed to quit my job after only six months of employment. In Korea, at least back then, professional employment was a lifetime event. No one quit or was let go of. You became part of the company's family. His first question was, "Is there something

I did wrong to cause you to quit?" He was so relieved when I told him about my plan to go abroad to study.

But I had to give up coming to the United States. Instead I enrolled for a graduate program at Inha Institute of Technology. There were only a few graduate programs in Korea during the late 1960s, and I was the only graduate student in my school. There were only a handful of professors with a PhD in Korea at that time. All PhD professors had received their degrees overseas.

My research program was on determining the reaction rate of acrylamide and styrene copolymerization. Acrylamide had to be purified by a process known as recrystallization. This was done under a boiling benzene solution carried out in a large, long-neck, glass flask fitted with a reflux condenser. The lab had no ventilation or fume hood. Now we know that benzene is a known carcinogen. A sub-ppm (part per million) level of benzene in air is harmful to humans. So I am still scratching my head, asking myself why I am still alive and healthy after being exposed to a many thousands of ppms of toxic benzene fume for nearly two years.

I still remember the accident scene vividly: It was a Saturday afternoon. All the students were gone, and the campus was peaceful. School opened for half a day on Saturdays in those days. The skies were blue, without a single cloud. It was a typical balmy, fall day in Korea.

As I had done many times before, I was boiling a benzene solution. Suddenly, the power went out. In those days, it was not unusual to have power outages. I knew I could stop and go home early, but I decided to finish as the benzene solution began to boil. I removed the reflux condenser, took the flask out of the electric heating mantle, and continued to boil it over a Bunsen burner. While I was holding the flask over the flame with one hand, I was looking out the windows, admiring the ineffable beauty of the verdant hills and trees with fall leaves.

As my eyes wandered leisurely from one scene to another, I began to notice from the corner of my eye, a yellowish, dancing

9

flame appearing on the window pane. "How strange," I murmured. As I turned my head back to the lab, I saw a flame pouring out of the flask. Instinctively, I let go of the flask. It shattered as it hit the floor. The benzene spread out instantly, and the whole floor turned into a sea of fire. Flames were shooting up wildly, producing black smokes.

I threw down several bottles of carbon tetrachloride on the floor in the directions where fires were burning fiercely. I knew it could extinguish fire, so I kept several bottles on the lab countertop just in case.

Soon the entire lab was engulfed by fire and smoke. It was very dark with smokes and fumes. I coughed, coughed, and coughed, and I was at the brink of passing out. An inner voice told me that if I did not get out immediately, I would not get out alive. Later I found out that the fumes were from phosgene, the poisonous gas used by the German military during the World War I to kill enemy soldiers.

I stumbled out of the building, coughing rapidly, gasping for air. As I ran out, a picture of the building as an inferno and of my face behind the bar flashed through my head. It was a large, multistory building that housed all the engineering departments. After I coughed and coughed some more, I dashed back to the lab. On the way in, I spotted a large, wooden box full of sand. I picked it up and carried it inside. I frantically scooped the sand out and threw it toward the fires. I then jumped out of the lab, coughed my lungs out, and went back again.

I do not remember how many times I repeated this task until I saw Doo-Hack, my high school buddy who was studying civil engineering, coming from the school library. Although we lived on opposite sides of town, we always walked together on our way home after school to the fork in the road where we went our separate way.

Doo-Hack joined me in combating the fire. When we finally knew the last flame had been extinguished, we ran out of the building, gasping and coughing, and then crashed onto the lawn, completely exhausted, breathing heavily. After a brief rest, we went back inside to see the damage. The lab was a mess. The floor was full of black stains and sand, and soot had gotten inside every open piece of lab ware—even inside of Erlenmeyer flasks. I noticed major damages to my professor's desk, his chair, and the cabinets. All the vinyl parts of the desk and chair were melted and deformed.

It was a daunting task to clean up. After several hours of cleaning, we felt spent and decided to quit for the day. We had another day to clean. Before leaving, we decided to take the sandbox back to where it had been. It was a large container still half full of sand. Doo-Hack and I crouched to pick it up, but we couldn't lift it. To this day, I wonder who was there beside me, helping me carry the sandbox into the room.

As a year or so passed by, the government loosened its policy on the byungjong status and ordered the byungjong men to undergo the physical again before they would be allowed to leave the country. If they passed the physical, they were to be sent straight to the military camp.

Although I had not done anything illegal to receive my previous byungjong status, I was not sure I wanted to go through the physical. I had borderline hypertension, and there was a fifty-fifty chance that it could go either way. Army doctors were now administering the physical exam, instead of the civilian doctors that I had done my earlier physical. All these things were on my mind.

I told one of my friends my dilemma. A few days later, he told me that he had discussed it with his uncle, who had promised that he could help me with my physical. It just so happened that he was based at the military medical center where my physical was to take place, but he was a colonel, not a doctor. I was told later that my parents had put up a large sum of money for his promise to help me fail my physical. *How could he, the uncle of one of my best friends, accept money?* I said to myself, disgusted. It was hurtful to know that my friend had let me down, although he may have been just as disgusted with his uncle. After he received the money, we lost contact with him.

I was scared on the day of the test. When the army doctor told me to come back that afternoon for a retest, I was even more scared. In that afternoon, after he removed the arm strap from me, he patted me on my back and said, "Study hard, and come back to help the country." He then told me the reason I was told to come back. He had suspected that I had taken a drug that would raise my blood pressure, seeing my extremely high blood pressure on my first test. He wanted to see my normal blood-pressure reading without the aid of a drug. That's when I realized why he had told me that he would take a urine sample. But I did not even know such a medicine existed.

Several days later, I went to the passport office to apply for my passport. They told me that they could not process it until they received my byungjong certificate. I went to the army medical center and asked a clerk if it had been sent. His answer was "It's on its way." I was happy that things were finally working out.

The next day, I took a train to Seoul from Incheon, where I lived. It took about an hour to get to Seoul and then a good walk to the passport office. The man behind the front desk told me that they had not received it yet. I went back to the Army Medical Center again on the following day and got the same story. I wanted to ask, "Why is it taking so long when both offices are in the same city and a little more than walking distance from each other." But that would have provoked his anger. Who knows what he would do? After all, the country was ruled by the military.

My approach was to show up every day until they got tired of seeing me or even felt pity for me. This ritual lasted several weeks. I complained to my oldest brother who lived in Seoul at that time. He told me that he would go and see what he could do. The next day, I went back to the passport office and, to my surprise, the clerk told me he had received it. A few days later, my brother told me that he had to give them money. "How naïve you are," he said with a sigh. I was relieved but at the same time hurt, thinking about all my wasted effort.

Finally my departure day came. My whole family, one of my mom's friends, and two of my friends came to the airport to say farewell. My mom was visibly happy. After taking many pictures, they all finally left, as my departure time was near.

I proceeded toward the gate. A man at the gate stopped me and wanted to see my passport and vaccination certificate. I handed them over to him. After glancing at them rather quickly, he said to me in a low, compassionate tone. "Oh, I am sorry, but you do not have all the required vaccinations." I was petrified. I had asked the nurse at the clinic, and she had told me that I was good to go. "Why didn't she examine my certificate more carefully?" I muttered.

The plane was about to leave. When I glanced at him, he looked concerned. Finally, he told me that he could help me. *How could he help me now?* I wondered. Then I felt relieved, thinking that he must have a medical instrument to examine folks like me on the spot. I was anxiously waiting for him to pull the instrument out of his desk drawer or somewhere. I did not know that he was also anxiously waiting for me to pull money out of my pocket.

He finally told me what he was waiting for. I said instantly, "I have no money."

He said, "US dollars would be okay."

"Oh, that is money, too," I murmured. As soon as he received the money, he stamped a seal on my certificate and permitted me to proceed through the gate. This experience has left a deep scar in my heart that has not been healed to this day.

CHAPTER 3

College in United States

The flight took me to Tokyo. I seated myself and closed my eyes. I could not take my mind off the incident that I'd just had. *How agonizing it must have been for the man to utter the M word in a country where it is not spoken but understood,* I thought. I was too naïve to understand his unspoken language.

The flight was short, and before my mind wandered much farther, my plane landed. At the Tokyo airport, I saw a color TV screen for the first time. I had been fascinated when I heard about color TVs, as they had not yet been introduced in Korea. However, I was not impressed, because the pictures did not look real but painted.

After waiting many hours, I was on my way to Fairbanks, Alaska. My flight was on a big Pan Am airplane, and all passengers were non-Koreans. I felt uneasy among so many people speaking languages I was not accustomed to hearing. As I was seated, I closed my eyes to try to sleep. Instead I was overcome by fear—fear of the unknown. I had sent a letter informing school of my departure date. However, I was not sure if they had received my letter. And if they did, had they done anything about it? Also, there was a general fear – fear of facing the uncertain future alone. This fear had been

15

with me all along, but suppressed by other pressing matters. Now, it surfaced and began to occupy my mind.

The plane landed at the Fairbanks Airport, and as I claimed my baggage, a tall, young man was waiting for me. He had come to pick me up in his VW beetle. It was two thirty in the morning. The air was clean and fresh, with an unfamiliar smell, yet it was pleasant to my nose. The land was so strange that I thought I'd landed on a different planet. It turned out that the tall, young man was an English student in my class.

We arrived at a tall building. My room was on the eighth floor. At the door, he dropped a key in my hand and left. By the time I opened my dorm room, sunlight was coming through the window. It was only four. I closed the drapes, which were thick, so they blocked most of the sunlight. But there was plenty still leaking through where the drapes met the wall. I lay down on the bed, and though I was sleepy, I did not think I could sleep in such a brightly lit room. But before long, I fell asleep.

I dreamt I was standing near the water's edge. In front of me was a beautiful yet mysterious lake, partially covered with fog. I could not see the other side clearly, but I knew I had to be there. I fretted, wondering how I could get there, so far away. I tried to flutter my arms in desperation as though they were wings. To my surprise, I found myself up in the air, flying. As I finally landed on the other side of the lake, I woke up.

How weird, I thought. I felt so strange finding myself in a room so unfamiliar, so far away from home. I opened the drapes, and sunlight shone through the windows brightly. I saw a wide-open plain stretching as far as my eyes could see. On the other side, far away, were layers of mountains covered with snow. It was nothing like I had even seen or imagined.

I stayed all day in my room, eating what I had brought. On the second day, I walked two hundred yards or so and came back, making sure that I could trace my footsteps back to my dormitory. On the third day, I walked more. It was mid-August. The campus was quiet, as most of students had gone. My food ran completely out on the third day, and my fear of being lost was overcome by my hunger.

I found myself in the school cafeteria, picking up a tray and utensils as the person in front of me did. I pointed at the vegetables on the display behind the glass as I walked by. The only food closely resembling the food I was familiar with was steamed vegetables. I sat at a table far away from anyone in the room. I glanced quickly at others to avoid making eye contact.

I was surprised and embarrassed when I noticed that the food on my tray was three or four times more than what others had in their trays. I glanced at one person to my right and then quickly turning my head to another person to my left, trying to learn how to use a fork. It was my first time using a fork, and I wanted to look as normal as possible.

During the next few days, I ate pretty much the same vegetables but a little less amount, although I could eat more. Each meal cost five to six dollars. Soon I realized that at that rate, my money would not last long. Yet school was still weeks away. I converted the dollars to Korean won in my head. Five to six dollars per meal was a huge sum of money in Korea. I could buy a good Korean meal for about thirty cents. Two hundred dollars minus the money I gave to the man at the airport was all I had. (Two hundred was the maximum amount allowed out of the country by the Korean government.) I found out later that other students got out a lot more than this amount. When I heard this, it fueled my frustration with my home country; the country where I had grown up was being eaten away by corruption. It seemed that I had grown up so much over the last few years and had seen so many ugly sides of my country.

To save money, I decided to find a grocery store and to cook for myself. There was a small kitchen on our dorm floor, and no one was there to use it. I found a country grocery store in the same way I found the cafeteria—by increasing my walking distance each passing day. It took me several days to spot the store. It was at the bottom of the hill, not far from the campus, as it turned out.

As I entered the store, I stood just inside the doorway and waited, as we did at grocery stores in Korea. We didn't pick up the items by ourselves in Korea back then. We told the storekeeper what we needed, and he or she brought our order to us.

I was standing there for what seemed to be an hour while muttering some bad words (of course, Korean). I came to realize that he was not about to leave his seat. Disgusted with his service, or nonservice, I went to him and I asked him for milk. He did not understand me. I said, "*Milk,*" a little louder. He shook his head. I raised my voice even higher, as if my voice was not loud enough. Finally, I spelled out the word. He still shook his head. So I repeated "M-I-L-K" several times, again a little louder each time. The outcome was still the same.

I began to feel helpless and upset, thinking, *How could he not know this simple word?* Then he said, "Oh, I got it" or something like that. I was so relieved. He then lumbered off toward the back of the store. Soon I saw him coming back with a lump of meat in his hand. I knew then that my life in the United States would not be an easy one. I bought that meat—not that I wanted it, but to be polite.

On the way into the store, I had seen dried beef strips in a clear plastic jar on the table. Written on the lid was "25 cents." *That jar holds a lot of beef jerky for only 25 cents,* I thought as I walked by. As I got ready to pay for the meat, I remembered the beef jerky, so I grabbed two jars. For the next few days, I was eating beef jerky for meals, since I had spent my meal allowance on beef jerky. I don't remember what I did with the meat.

School finally opened. I was advised to take a microbiology course required by the environmental engineering department—a 400-level, advanced undergraduate course. I had an engineering degree in Korea, and biology and microbiology were not my cup of tea. In fact, I had never taken a microbiology course, let alone biology.

In the class, the professor spoke nonstop from beginning to end. So other students kept busy jotting notes nonstop from beginning to end. To me, he might as well have been a Martian who had just landed on earth, and speaking to us. I spent most of my time in the class just sitting there, letting my mind wander. Fear—fear of coming home disgraced—was what occupied my mind the most.

Strangely enough, the only word I could hear clearly in the first few classes was *Korea*. *Why is he saying that word?* I wondered. Years passed before I figured out why. I had heard him wrong. He was saying *career*, not *Korea*—the one word I thought I understood perfectly.

I studied until the wee hours pretty much every day, mostly studying microbiology. I gazed at the winter skies lit with eerie auroras as I walked a lonely walk back in a dark, cold night to my dorm from library. The auroras seemed to understand my plight.

You may ask, "Why didn't you study in your room, saving all the trouble of walking to and from the library on cold nights?" Ah, I was not making my life any harder on purpose. Although I was on a male-only floor, the dormitory was co-ed—a wild place, even on weekdays. I was not used to seeing scantily clad women running around, giggling and screaming wildly. I was dumbstruck when I first saw a woman popping out of the men's room as I entered.

Also, I had a roommate, an American student, and I was uncomfortable in his presence. He had a big hunting knife; I had never seen a knife quite like it. Back in Korea, no one had or was allowed to carry a knife, except a small pencil-sharpening knife. I knew that only criminals carried such a menacing knife. That thought evoked much fear. For the first several nights, I slept with one eye open, so to speak.

Memorizing the tongue-twisting names of microorganisms from the textbook was so, so hard. To make matters even worse, the exam materials were all from the lecture. It turned out that the textbook was just one of the teacher's references. I got a C on that course— okay for an undergraduate, but a failing grade for a graduate.

When I spoke, I had to speak very fast, so I was told to speak slowly. Alas, they did not understand my problem: I had to think in Korean first and then convert it to English. And then I had to spit it out fast for fear of losing my just-composed English sentence. Often I was preparing for my answer before I heard the whole question, so that I'd have more composing time.

I knew all along I had a mediocre brain. My strong point, if I had one, was persistence. The old adage "Persistence will eventually triumph" did not seem to apply; my effort did not bring about good academic results. Many a time, I wanted to go back home. Life there was so much simpler. But I knew I could not go back. My parents, particularly my mom, were so proud of me. I could not face her. I was well aware that having one of her children study abroad was her joy, and she would brag about it even to any stranger who cared to listen. I came to a realization that my coming to America was as much hers as mine, and I needed her approval to go back.

Furthermore, the painful experiences I had gone through over the years would have been in vain. I remembered the agony of mistakenly taking the English *yoohak* exam twice, even though I passed on the first one, and not retaking the Korean history exam, thinking that I had passed the first one. This mistake had delayed my departure one more year. And many bad things occurred during that year.

During my second year in Alaska, life got a little easier. Microbiology was behind me. Thankfully, the C on my microbiology did not affect my research assistant status. And I met more students. Several Chinese graduates, one Korean undergraduate freshman, a student from India, and three Americans were among the students I had meals with regularly.

My friend Mary Spires was a fun girl to be with, but studying was not her strong suit. Later she left the school to live in Richmond, Virginia, with her long-lost father. Her parents divorced when she was very young, and she had grown up with her mom in Talkeetna, Alaska. Her departure was kind of a bittersweet.

Early in September 1972, I was accepted into the PhD program in environmental engineering at the University of Florida. My flight was rerouted to the Eielson Air Force Base near Fairbanks due to snow, because the Fairbanks Airport was closed. Eielson had a heated runway.

The flight took me to New York's Kennedy Airport. I had to take a city bus to go to another airport (La Guardia, I think). The bus was packed and noisy, like buses I used to ride in Korea. I wanted to stay close to the driver, but I was standing in the back of the bus. If I missed the airport, I would miss the flight to Gainesville, and I would be lost on some New York street. That thought evoked a deep fear.

My mom traveled to United States several times over the years, and she knew no English. She must have had many incidents like this. *How much fear must she have felt?* I often wonder.

She once told me a story: "At an airport, I did not know where the restroom was. I could no longer hold it," she said. "I grabbed someone and pointed my finger at the area of my body." When she told this story, I laughed and cried inside at the same time. I flashed back to my memory of the fear I had endured on the bus ride in New York to the airport en route to Gainesville, Florida, not that long before.

When I deplaned at the Gainesville Airport, it was pouring. The humidity and heat were unbearable. I felt like my head was just inside an oven. For several days, I slept on one of the benches scattered around the campus until I found a low-rent apartment.

School was much easier as time progressed. After several moves, I settled in George Seagle Hall, a co-op on University Avenue. The rent was low, but it required chores, like doing dishes. I stayed there until I finished school. I cherished my time there, meeting many students and doing chores with them.

I remember a time there when I had flu. I was so sick and weak that I could not get up and eat meals. For the first time, I was thinking about my death, and I was horrified when I imagined no one finding me until my decayed body began to stink. I thought about home, and wished I were there. My mom would be there beside me. After four or five days in bed with no food, a strange inner voice told me, "Get up and eat if you want to live."

Toward my third year, my course work was completed, and I could devote all my time to my research. My daily routine was going to my office/lab after dinner and staying until three or four in the morning. Then I came home and slept until around noon. I chose to work during those odd hours because it was quiet and all the analytical instruments were available.

The research was on the absorption of hexavalent chromium in activated carbon. At that time, the toxicity of hexavalent chromium had been established, and tighter EPA discharge limits were to go into effect. The outcome of this research would help the industry meet the EPA limit.

My research did not progress well—in fact, it hit a snag. It makes sense that if you add more carbon to a chromium solution, more chromium would be absorbed in the carbon. But I was getting the opposite result. I visited several chemistry professors, and they all gave me a predictable response: I must be doing something wrong—probably due to contamination because of sloppy laboratory practices, for example.

Finally, my research came to a standstill. Half a year went by with absolutely no progress. Frustration was mounting. The thought about changing the research project came up frequently. It was hard to drop it and start something new all over again. That goes against my ingrained beliefs. "Grinding it out" fits my personality.

I was so elated when I found the explanation for this unexplainable phenomenon. I don't want to bore you with the details. Just know that my research picked up steam. Now I could see light at the end of the tunnel.

CHAPTER 4

Career and Family

I was offered a postdoctoral assignment at Virginia Tech in Blacksburg, Virginia. After I defended the dissertation successfully, I bought a used 1972 Opel for $1,200. I thought I had some money left to pay the first month's rent. I crammed the car with books and personal belongings and headed for Manassas, Virginia, where there was a field research station.

Before my work even began, I had to ask for an advance, as I was short on cash to pay the first month's rent plus the deposit. The landlord demanded two months of rent to cover the deposit.

There I met my wife. I had dated her for four months or so before we got married. I still remember the night after I met her. I drove to Arlington, Virginia, to see her. Just before I arrived at her apartment, my Opel lost its brakes. I had to explain to her why I had to be with her until after midnight—highway traffic would be much lighter later at night. She had to go to work next morning. I did not know if she believed my story. She might have thought that that was some excuse I was using to stay with her longer.

I decided to use Highway 50 instead of I-66 so that I could drive slowly. On the way home, I got pulled over. "Why are you going so slow?" the policeman asked. He had me do a test drive, and I pulled the emergency brake so hard that my hand was tingling for several days.

I was bracing myself for him to order me to go and check into a nearby hotel, and I saw a hotel sign right up the hill. But he let me go. I felt so relieved, because I had no means to pay for a hotel stay. It took me three hours to get to my apartment in Manassas; normally it was a thirty- to forty-minute drive.

We were married on July 2, 1977. The ceremony lasted only a few minutes. Only my brother, my soon-to-be wife's brother, his wife, and of course, the judge were present. We did not have money for a formal wedding. Besides, we did not have any friends to invite.

Money was tight, and we lived paycheck to paycheck. After brief employment at a consulting firm, I got laid off. I was to start a new project, but unexpectedly the contract was awarded to another company.

Around this time, my wife told me that she was pregnant. With no insurance, we decided to have the baby by natural childbirth. We attended a Lamaze class regularly.

I often wondered if it was a right thing to bring a child into this world—into a white society. My life had been difficult, far from what I had dreamt of. I often wondered about the wisdom of coming here.

I remember my mom saying that in my field I would be highly sought-after in Korea, and she often urged me to go back. I thought about that a lot. Could I be happier there? The painful experiences I'd had there haunted me. Yet I did not want my children to go through life handicapped as second-class citizens. I wasn't sure if my wife wanted to go back either. All this occupied my mind.

My wife started having contractions sometime after midnight. I called the midwife. She told me that she was not contractually obligated to come and help with the delivery, as my wife had passed her expected due date by almost two weeks. I called the clinic, and it was a horrible several hours before two midwives arrived. All I could do was boil water, though I did not know what I was supposed to do with a pot of hot water.

At around eleven in the morning, she gave birth to a cute, healthy baby boy, and we named him Paul. About a month or so later, she checked into a hospital and stayed three days due to childbirth-related complications. I tried to bottle feed him, but he refused the bottle and cried nonstop at every waking moment for two solid days. It was heartbreaking to watch him crying so much for so long, and I did not know how to help him.

We did not decide to breastfeed Paul; we simply did not have money to buy formula. My wife found work at Pam's Donuts to support us, which as on the Beauregard Street and Little River Turnpike intersection, not far from our apartment in Alexandria.

After a year of joblessness, I found a job at Hittman Associates, a midsized consulting firm in Columbia, Maryland. In its heyday, some four hundred technical people worked there, I was told. I worked on an EPA project to assess the impacts of coal liquefaction on the environment.

Commuting between Alexandria and Columbia wore me out. It took a little more than an hour to travel one way on a good day. However, bad days outnumbered good days. I was tired all the time. My wife thought I had a brain tumor or something. I blamed the driving, but it could have been from the job stress, or both.

After a year of commuting, we moved to an apartment in Columbia. Soon after, I got a telephone call from my brother in Korea that my father had passed away after a long illness. He had throat cancer from smoking all his life. I was not able to go to Korea, since we did not have money to purchase the airfare. We had no idea who to borrow money from. My brother and my wife's brother's family were all struggling financially.

My father had worked hard all his life for his family. The thought that I was unable to see him one last time weighed on my mind heavily. Many things that had happened to me since I came to the United States were outside the realm of my imagination, unprepared for, and contrary to my dreams. I realized that my dream of getting a PhD and the resulting good life were in no way close to what I had envisioned back in Korea. I wished I could undo what I had done. My wife told me that she was pregnant again. We had insurance, and we decided the baby would be born in the hospital. We learned the hard way that natural childbirth was not for faint-hearted folks. After dinner one evening, she told me she was having contractions. On the way to the hospital, which was not far from our apartment, she said she felt fine and told me to take her back home. We were on the overpass just crossing over Highway 29, and since we were about halfway point to the hospital, we decided to drive to the hospital.

A nurse came out and told me that she would have a baby shortly. At exactly midnight, we had a baby girl, Tonia. She was so small and so cute, in a different way from Paul. We could not decide on her birthday. Should it be on January 22 or January 23. The doctor finally decided it for us. He picked the 22nd. His logic was that she was halfway out at midnight. He could have easily said the 23rd, since the other half was still in.

Tonia was formula fed; breastfeeding was not popular back then. Also, we could afford to buy formula. She was so easy to take care of. She slept through the night. When Paul was her age, he'd wake up every so often for Mom's milk. I was so tired from the lack of sleep.

We had only one car, so my wife had to wait until I came back from work to go grocery shopping. Often I came home late. On several occasions, we went shopping after dinner while she was asleep at home, because we were sure she would not wake up. We found out later that leaving a child in a house alone was against the law. As I look back, I am amazed how careless we were. My apologies to my daughter for our recklessness.

I felt somewhat secure with my new job. I went to a Sears store and applied for a credit card, though I don't know why I wanted it. Perhaps, subconsciously, I wanted to fit into the American culture. I thought I would get it for the asking, since I had no money but no debt. Sears disapproved my application on the spot: no credit history—a cut-and-dried case. I found myself saying, "I should be in debt to borrow money, so that I could be more in debt? Those Sears people are not so bright."

At about that time, OPEC declared embargo on oil shipment to United States. We could get only five gallons of gas after waiting several hours in a long line in front of a gas station. At another time, gas stations were restricted to sell the gas based on the car license number. On an odd calendar day, you could buy gas if your car had the odd license number.

In the aftermath of the OPEC embargo, the Carter administration had created the new, cabinet-level Energy Mobilization Board.

Do you know the difference between coal and crude oil? One is a solid and the other one liquid. That is how most folks would answer. Aside from this glaring difference, coal contains mostly carbon. Oil contains carbon too, but also many hydrogen atoms. So the coal liquefaction process basically is nothing more than cooking coal in a hydrogen atmosphere, which adds hydrogen to it. Germany produced oil from coal through this process during the World War II, when crude oil could not be imported. So we were borrowing the old German technology.

My job at Hittman was to participate in an EPA-sponsored project to characterize and quantify the pollutants generated by this process. The EPA was to set the pollution discharge guidelines based on the results

An oil company built a fifty-ton-capacity pilot plant in Fort Lewis, Washington. If you see the actual facility, you might think it is a large refinery complex. I made many trips and sometimes stayed in the Tacoma/Seattle area for a month. Isn't Fort Lewis a military base? Why in the military base? Ah! This was to circumvent EPA regulations. At that time, the EPA had no jurisdictions over military bases.

As the plant had more outage than operating time, we had a lot of free time and did a lot of sightseeing. We even went to Canada. I still remember the trouble I got myself into. Two coworkers and I drove to Canada one morning, but on the way back that afternoon, we were stopped by a US customs official. I was asked many questions: How long have you have been in Canada. Are you a US citizen? What are you doing in Canada? I could not provide a document to back up my answers. Two coworkers were not questioned. I did not expect a welcome mat, but treating me as a crime suspect was disheartening. Why were they targeting me only? You could call it *profiling*, but *discrimination* would probably a more fitting word.

You've heard of the government's wasteful spending. I've witnessed it myself. It seemed that every year or so, a new EPA program manager was introduced, and that new manager would want to change the scope of the program. That kind of change always meant more money and more time for Hittman. So the project was perpetuated.

I was project engineer and was responsible for dolling out man-hours and work assignments to my team members. They used up all the hours before completing their assigned tasks and asked for more hours. My boss, an old physics professor, had told me that there wasn't enough money left for overtime. So I had to do my team members' work without getting overtime. I learned later that he was coming to the office every weekend, charging overtime against our project while he was doing his own personal business. He was even praised by Mr. Hittman, the company owner, for his exemplary working habit.

It was so frustrating. I started having a constant migraine. I was tired and wanted to stay home and rest over the weekend. My wife was cooped up at home, taking care of our three- and one-year-old. She wanted to go out over the weekend to a shopping mall or anyplace away from home. This was putting stress in our marriage.

Knowing that my job would be around for the foreseeable future, we bought our first house, a small townhouse in Elkridge, Maryland, just off US Highway 1. We had a mortgage with payments that went up each year along with the principal. It was like this: the more we pay, the more we owe. How could this be possible? It was an era when the typical interest rate on a loan was 20 percent. Our interest on my mortgage was 14.9 percent. The lender told us that we were getting a good deal.

Based on our income, our monthly payment fell short of meeting the interest on our borrowed money (the principal). I think this was called "negative amortization." The mortgage industry came up with this creative loan to help unqualified home buyers qualify to buy homes. The idea behind this is that your pay would go up each year, so you could pay more in interest payment as the year progresses. And at some future point, your monthly payment would exceed the interest you owed. But who could guarantee my pay would go up and how much each year? I thought this was a rip-off.

My biweekly check was meager. This may be a little stretch, but I probably was the lowest paid employee holding a PhD in America. It was not in my character to negotiate my pay with my employer. The interviewer asked me what annual salary I had in mind, and I quickly added a few thousand dollars to the pay I received from my previous employer. I did not want my pay to be a barrier to my employment. How could I even bring a pay increase up for discussion when I already felt so indebted to the employer offering me the job? He told me his company could add a few thousand dollars more, but, of course, he was not generous.

We were not broke, but we had trouble making both ends meet. One day, to my surprise, a Sears credit card was in our mailbox. I thought, *Why now?* When I could afford to buy, they did not want me to have one. Now that we were broke, they wanted us to have one. Before I knew it, I was using the credit card more than I wanted. *Those folks knew exactly how to put us in a hole and to keep us there for good,* I thought.

Ronald Reagan's election to the presidency in 1980 was a turning point for us. Reagan fulfilled his campaign promise to shrink the government and reduce regulations. He was particularly harsh on the EPA and its overreaching regulatory power. He abolished the Energy Mobilization Board, one of Jimmy Carter's presidential centerpieces. Reagan also opposed the idea of producing oil from coal, stating that we had plenty of oil, and it was only a matter of pumping it out. Ann Gorsuch, the EPA administrator, buttered up Reagan by announcing the reduction of the EPA budget by half. In the wake of all that brouhaha, the EPA stopped funding our project. Basically, they broke the contract. One thing I learned was that you don't sue the government for breaking the contract. I became unemployed again. By the time I left the company, there were less than twenty people working there. It was near the end of its run. It had put all its eggs in one EPA basket.

My wife went back to working at a donut shop. Inflation was rampant, and jobs were hard to come by.

A year had passed when I got a call from EG&G. It was a large company and had many subsidiaries, one of which was a consulting arm where I would be working. I later found out that this company invented the device that detonated the atomic bombs that were dropped on Japan.

We loaded our two kids in our old Opel and headed for Morganton, West Virginia. The road to Morganton was mountainous. I had a hard time ordering our lunch at a Long John Silver's, as I could not hear well due to my popped ears.

My interview went well, and they offered me a Job. My pay was considerably better than my paycheck at Hittman. Of course, I was elated, yet unsure of the future there. This would be my third consulting firm. Consulting firms tend to hire when they get a new contract and lay off when the project is finished. I was tired of being laid off.

In the week that followed, I got a call from Duke Power in Charlotte. Their pay offer was not as good as EG&G's, but my main concern was job security, not pay. So I accepted. I contacted EG&G and told them that I had thought over my decision and had decided not to accept the offer. I thought, *What a turnaround! I was almost begging for a job. Now I am turning it down.*

Before even ten minutes went by after I hung up the phone with EG&G, the phone rang. It was from Duke Power. The person I had talked with before was on the line. He started out saying, "I am very sorry, but apparently you did not pass the psychological exam. I should have checked into this first. I am sorry." The first thing that crossed my mind was that I had two jobs a few minutes ago, and now I had no job.

But he continued. "You can come back and take another test, of course; the company will pay for the cost of your trip. I am sure you will pass, but your employment is contingent on passing the second exam"

What kind of oxymoronic statement is he uttering? I thought while listening to him. In the end, I agreed to go down.

After I hung up the phone, I summoned all my guts, called EG&G, and told my interviewer that I would like to reconsider and accept the offer. I could hear his elated voice on the other end of line. I knew that I needed this job to fall back on if I failed the second test with Duke.

The exam lasted almost half a day. It included many silly questions, like "Do you love your mother? When you stand on the cliff, do you feel like jumping off?" Many were same questions but worded differently. So I was careful not to contradict myself.

After the exam, I went to see the person I had talked with over the phone. He was a department head, and he apologized again as soon as I introduced myself. I asked, "How long do I have to wait to know the result?"

To my dismay, he nonchalantly said, "A month or so." I would accept this in a heartbeat if it were the only job offer I had. I told him that if he did not let me know in the next few days, I would not be interested. I could not afford to be unemployed for another month.

I felt uneasy at the thought that I had been chasing after two wild geese and I might end up losing both in the process. A few days later, I was surprised and then worried when I got a call from Duke Power informing me that I had passed the test. I learned that Duke had to call Chapel Hill and give my answers over the phone. Normally, they mailed tests to the school, which reported the results back to Duke. That's why the process usually took a month or so. The caller told me that it was the first time they had done that. I was thinking, *Why did they go out of their way to do this? Do they need my expertise so badly? Did my bluffing do the trick?* I concluded the department head felt bad about his mistake.

Did I say calling EG&G to turn down the offer after accepting it was hard? It was even harder to call again to tell them that I'd like that job back. Now I had to call them to turn down again? I knew that I was not up to that task. I thought about not calling them and just not showing up to work, remembering my older brother at the Children's Hour on a Christmas Eve way back in Korea.

Back then, we had a Children's Hour every Christmas Eve. It included songs, dances, and dramas. I was about seven or eight, and my brother was about nine or ten. He was confident, even brash at times, for his age. I was opposite: timid and diffident.

The Children's Hour began with a short prayer, and my brother was to say it to lead the program. He had spent many hours memorizing it. The church was filled with the congregation plus unbelievers who came to this once a year. My mom was so proud of him. We all hung our heads and closed our eyes while he began the prayer. In the middle of it, he fell silent. It took a good while for the whole congregation to realize that he was not standing on the podium. If I were in his place, I would probably have been standing there crying.

I finally called EG&G to explain the situation. The person at the other end of the line was very understanding. I felt so good that I had called. I did not want to act like my older brother, who ran away when he was in a bind.

Duke was so different from any other consulting firm I had worked for. On my first day of work, I heard my new boss yelling at one of my coworkers. Their offices were across the hall from each other. My office was two doors down from my boss's office. I later asked the coworker what he had done to deserve that kind of treatment. He said, "Nothing really."

"I should have taken the other job," I murmured to myself.

By far, my boss was one of the most awful people I have ever met. However, to his credit, he was obnoxious pretty much to everyone. Although he was not as bad toward me, I wonder how I put up with him for so long.

I met many nice people there over the years. I did not learn until several years later that my job had been on the chopping block but was saved at the last minute by two hourly workers, who had no influence. Some twenty year ago, Duke Power was riding on a deregulation bandwagon, cutting operating costs to the bone. Cutting operating costs and downsizing are the same thing— euphemisms for *layoff.* Two technicians from the chemistry lab at Allen Steam Station were following the visiting vice president's footsteps, pleading him not to let me go.

I have many more heart-warming stories like this. However, all these good memories were overshadowed by my unpleasant experiences with my boss. On a bright note, I became his boss later, although it did not last long.

I am prone to mistakes. I have had more than my share of mistakes in the past. As such, I have an aversion to those who cannot admit their mistakes, like this boss.

Of many unpleasant encounters with him, I still remember this one vividly: While we were doing boiler chemical cleaning at Allen Steam Station in Belmont, North Carolina, one of the valve gaskets blew out, and we had to wait until it got repaired. While waiting, I came across a neatly handwritten sheet on a table. It was a corrosion coupon testing procedure my boss had written. Out of boredom, I was leisurely glancing through the procedure. As I handed it over to him, I said, "I could be wrong, but I found an error in the procedure, and could you double check your—?"

Before I had even finished my sentence, he hit the roof. "This procedure has been used for the last ten years, and there is nothing wrong with it," he retorted, and stormed out of the room. I thought, *Stupid me. Why did I bring that up?* Not even ten minutes passed, and

I saw him coming through the door with a coy smile. He approached me and said awkwardly, "I must have been thinking of something else while I was writing this procedure."

I wanted to say, "So, all the results for the past ten years were no good," but I said nothing. *Don't kick the dog when it is down*, I thought.

Another incident I cannot forget happened in the early 1990, I think. Belews Creek Power Plant in Walnut Cove, North Carolina, was losing 6 to 7 million dollars each year due to turbine deposits. This was the one of the largest power plants in United States, with two gigantic steam turbines. Deposits on turbine blades as thin as a few microns meant a major turbine efficiency drop, costing the company millions of dollars.

Turbine deposit sample analysis indicated that the deposit material was aluminum, which had passed through a series of water purification processes and found its way to the boiler. I found a simple process to remove this contaminant by injecting a small amount of polyelectrolyte into the filtration unit. I was elated that it worked so well at so little cost. The station decided to install a permanent injection system.

A week or so later, my supervisor said to me, "John, I know you are busy with other projects, so I decided to take you off this project and give it to a new person who has just been transferred to our group." I was not happy, but I did not think much of it. Not until several months later did I see a full-page picture of my boss and the new person standing in front of a stream turbine on the cover page of the company's annual stockholders' report. The report highlighted my boss's exemplary work and dedication, which had led to saving the company millions of dollars. I felt sick to my stomach knowing that a human being can go that low for fame and recognition.

I still fondly remember working with David Brindle, from our design engineering department. He looked a lot older than his age because of his premature white hairs. My coworkers used to tease me, asking, "Where's your dad?" I knew he was a model

Christian—one who does good deeds but says little about them. Knowing how I was treated by my boss, he submitted an application without my knowledge for an annual Excellence Award, listing for my contribution. He told me later that it was not accepted. It was comforting to know that there are still many good people around me when I seek solace.

My wife and I bought our first brand-new car, a Honda Civic wagon, in Maryland a few days before we moved to Charlotte. My wife had told me that she did not want to be seen in this rundown Opel. I had to show my employment paper at the dealership for them to approve the loan. The interest was an eye-popping 18 percent.

The winter of that year was very cold. Paul was six years old, and he was all excited about the snow, although he had seen it before when we were in Maryland. He came running in from outside, saying, "Dad, Dad, I removed snow off your car." He wanted me to come out and look. I was happy at the thought that he had become old enough to help me with chores. Sure enough, he had done it with a shovel. Oh no! But I praised him.

As time progressed at Duke, I felt, for the first time, secure in my job. My wife was doing her best to keep both of the children dressed properly. She made many pretty dresses for our daughter over the years—not so much for enjoyment but to save money. We did not want our kids to think they were poor and inferior.

After losing her husband, my mom visited the United States to see us often. She stayed with my younger brother for most of her stay, as he was doing well financially and lived in a large house. Also, there was a large Korean community as well as churches in the Washington suburbs.

While I was attending a conference in Pittsburgh, I got a phone call from my brother in Gaithersburg, Maryland. He told me that Mom was gravely ill, so I flew to Washington, DC, to see her.

A year before, she had undergone colon cancer surgery to remove a malignant tumor. Doctor had given her a clean bill of health. *How could the tumor spread so fast?* I wondered. *Why did she not see the doctor earlier?* Her cancer was in a late stage and had spread all over her body. Her doctor recommended against any further surgery. She had to leave the hospital to go home to die. It was so sad to think about.

Feelings were pouring out of me unchecked: memories of her sacrifice through all those years, raising her seven children. I started blaming myself for not being on her side when frictions developed between my mom and my wife, blaming my brother for not being diligent about taking her to see the doctor, and then blaming my wife. Why couldn't she get along with Mom?

I was at her bedside, reading a technical paper I had brought with me in preparation for a graduate school environmental class. I was teaching at UNC Charlotte as a part-time instructor. My mom was in and out of consciousness. When she awakened, she saw me reading and asked me in an almost inaudible voice what I was doing. I told her I was an instructor, and I was preparing for a college class. She smiled faintly and urged me to go on home and prepare for the class.

My becoming a college professor had been her dream. I knew, then, that I had made her happy, although I was a temporary, part-time instructor, which was a far cry from being a full-time professor

I went home not knowing when she would pass away. A week later, my brother called. I knew right away what his call was about. It was so hard to believe that my mom would not be around anymore. Suddenly, the whole world seemed to be an empty and desolate place to live in. She was a hub of our family. All family communications filtered through her. She had kept us close. I knew our family would be drifting more apart with our mom gone. I also knew that she took with her all the secrets and untold stories I had always wanted to hear. I wish I had started writing this manuscript earlier, while mom was with me. She could certainly jog my blurred childhood memory.

Our son Paul has always been reserved and avoids conflicts. On the contrary, Tonia is outgoing and confrontational at times. For instance, if I ask both of them to do a chore, Paul would say, "Later," and Tonia would say, "I won't do it," though they both meant the same thing. These earlier traits stayed with them as they grew up.

When Tonia was in the first through third grades, she often threatened to call 911. I do not remember what triggered her to say that.

The schools seem to have rules for those few parents who abuse their children, but those rules apply to every parent. These rules can create unintended consequences, including causing the parents to feel alienated from their own children. I am sure it was not Tonia's doing, but the school's doing through her. But it hurt me to hear those threatening words from my own daughter. I don't remember that I ever put my hands on my children. Their mom would vouch for that.

When Tonia turned fifteen and a half, she told me, "I need to have a car." Two years before, we had bought Paul a new Ford Ranger that was stripped down—manual transmission with no air—after spending several days in frustration trying to find a good used car. Tonia continued. "Why can't you buy me a car? I only ask you to buy me a used car. Remember, you bought your son a brand-new car." She called her brother "your son" whenever she was upset.

Finally, I said, "I do not understand why you don't want to ride the school bus. All the school buses I see on the road are not even half full."

Oh, she was so upset! "Do you want me to ride with kids?" she retorted.

I was about to say, "Aren't you still a kid?" but I did not, for a fear of an outburst. So I said, "If I ever became the principal of your school, do you know what I would do on my first day of my job?"

"What?" she asked.

"I would have the student parking lot bulldozed and turned it into a flower garden."

"Dad, I would not do that if I were you," said she.

"Why? I am a school principal, and I can do what I want."

"No, I don't want you to get shot dead.

Oh my god, I thought. I knew I was still living in a world that no longer existed, but I did not want to leave that world for a new world that I was foreign to.

She had many cars afterward. When she asked for what may have been the third or fourth car, I replied in a half-annoyed voice, not particularly seeking a response from her, "Why do I have to buy you so many cars?"

"Because you were buying me all junk cars. Remember, you bought your son a new car," she replied.

"Oh, how true and untrue," I murmured to myself, remembering that the work done on two separate occasions was on an overheated, cracked engine head due to her operating her car with little or no engine oil.

I knew Paul would graduate college without much fanfare. I was worried about Tonia. She had many friends who were not attending college. As my parents had done, I wanted to see my two children finish college—not necessarily for a better job, but to broaden their horizons. Perhaps this is my way of justifying my being in school so long.

Over the years, Tonia gave us many joys as well as surprises— many of them good surprises, some not so good. Oh, how happy and proud we were when we heard her name announced over the PA system and saw her stepping forward to receive the Young Author award at Independent High. Another happy moment was when we found a letter in our mailbox. It was from UNC, Chapel Hill. Oh, how scared we were to open the envelope, not knowing if it was a rejection or an acceptance letter.

Tonia has great potential to be a good writer. I knew that all along, with her being editor of the Independent High newspaper and so on. Dr. Sontag, her UNC English professor, wrote a letter to us saying that too.

I have no bucket list. I don't need one, because I have only one wish: to find myself, someday, wandering in a bookstore, hearing myself bragging about the book that I hold in my hand to whoever cares to listen—just the way my mom did about my yoohak. Unlike Paul, Tonia had a wild side. Many a night, we stayed awake until she came home. Amid all that, I knew she would make it through okay. I was worried more about Paul. He was inward, reserved, and passive at times. I still wonder how much he has struggled to fit in a culture unkind to those not of their kind. I faced many hurdles as an adult. How difficult it must have been for a child to face those huddles? I feel closer to my son than to my daughter, only because I see myself in him. When I look at my daughter, I see an American girl with an Asian face.

Most of time, Paul announced to us what he was going to do—not necessarily asking for our permission. Several years ago, my wife and I traveled to Alexandria, Virginia, where he lived, as we had often done in the past. One evening, during our conversation over dinner, he mentioned casually that he was thinking about quitting his job and doing some traveling overseas. I thought he wasn't serious but was simply expressing his desire to do it someday. A month or so passed, and he called us asking us if he could store his belongings in our home. And I remembered what he had said over the dinner. He has been outside the United States for almost three years now. I wanted him to get married and settle down, but I realize that it is his life, not mine to meddle with.

Tonia usually informed us of what she had already done. For example, several years ago, she e-mailed us to inform us of her wedding. She said that only a few of her friends were invited; she did not want us to come all the way to Alaska. She said that she had been with her new husband for several years and that the wedding was just a formality.

Tonia always had a way of saying things that swayed me, though sometimes not wholeheartedly, to believe her version of any story. But this one was different. I felt disowned, abandoned. They say that time heals all wounds. I am not sure if I will ever get over this one.

My wife took this in stride and urged me to keep the communication open so as not to lose a daughter.

A couple of years back, Tonia e-mailed me to tell us that she was working for Alaska Airlines as a flight attendant. Because of the many stories she had told us, I thought she had liked her previous job. In it, she had helped Alaskan natives who did not have a high school diploma prepare for the equivalency exam.

She told me that she caught her program director misusing the government money for her own benefit. She confronted her about it, but was told later that her yearly contract would not be renewed. On her last day, because very popular among her coworkers, they threw a big going-away party. She received gifts from them as well as from the program director. As the director handed her present to her, she pushed it back to her, saying, "I don't want a gift bought with government money."

When I heard this, I was proud of her, yet worried. In her lifetime, she will encounter many more situations like this one. In such situations, I have chosen to be silent, to look the other way, because my family and mortgage came first. I admire her courage but wonder how much she will have to pay for it. And will she become like me? I hate even the thought of it.

Over the course of our marriage, we bought many houses—five to be exact. Do you know what all those houses have in common? Large living rooms. Oh, disregard our tiny first townhouse in Elkridge, Maryland. They also were all new.

We had our share of arguments during each purchase. My dream home had many small rooms, some of which are windowless, where I could hide from the outside world. She wanted a house with a big, open space, with large windows and a few rooms. So you can see our problem. We could not find a home with all those features.

I must confess that she is years ahead of me in many things, especially in the area of art and esthetics, and it would take years for me to catch up. It may have been in 1997. One day, she told me that she wanted to move. At first I thought she was joking, but she was not. I said, "What?" I could not believe my ears. "We've just settled in," I said. "Now I can begin to love my house: the interior, the colors of our tiles, the carpets, and all that you picked."

But she said, "We've been here for almost ten years. I am beginning to get tired of this house." Was she saying that her artistic view had changed over time? *Oh my, I am in for big trouble,* I thought. That year we moved to our Huntersville home. It seems that I have never been allowed to catch up with her in the area of home decor and aesthetics.

CHAPTER 5

Retirement

My company was merging with a Midwest utility company. It was offering a voluntary separation package to reduce the workforce as a result of merger. I thought about my age and the one-year salary they were offering. It was a rude awakening to find out that I was the oldest person in my department. Also, I thought about the layoff potential if I did not take the package, however remote that possibility was.

Our department technical manager's background was business. He had been hired during the electric utility deregulation era. During that time, Duke was replacing most of the engineering managers with ones with business backgrounds.

Do you remember the Enron scandal? Duke envied Enron and was trying hard to emulate the now defunct energy company. That once reputable company was disgraced as result of dubious and illegal energy trading. Enron had gotten out of the energy-producing business and had become an energy-trading company. It was accused of creating artificial energy shortages to jack up prices. Duke was also involved in this scheme, and our company stock started falling precipitously in a matter of a few weeks. Many stockholders, including me, lost lifelong savings. I had most of my 401K money in Duke's stocks.

43

During that period, I complained to our department's tech manager that many new water-treatment plants were constructed of substandard materials. I further warned him about the potential consequences of increased operating costs due to equipment failures and the resulting forced outages.

I was hoping that he would agree with me, if nothing else. Instead, he gave me a lecture. "John, we do not make money by selling power. We make money by moving assets." I was not sure of exactly what he was saying. Observing my puzzled look, he added, "We are not building the plants to keep but to sell. We will operate them for a few years until we find buyers." Before then, I had been proud of being part of a well-respected company. Now I was ashamed. It took many decades and many dedicated people to build a good reputation. It took less than a year for a greedy few to destroy it.

I could almost read a "you're still here?" look on his face as we passed each other in the hall. He got his job through his connection to yet another incompetent vice president, who got that job the same way. He was known to be unpredictable, as most incompetent people are. So I was not sure I wanted to take a chance. I was well aware that if I did not take the package and I got laid off, I would receive a standard layoff package, which would amount to little. Besides, I wanted to leave a company on my own terms for the first time. It was a hard decision, and I wrestled with it for a month, until the day the offer was to expire. I decided to retire after working for nearly twenty-five years. It seemed that not long before I had been looking desperately for a job.

I had many things in mind that I wanted to do after retirement. But they were not well defined; they were more like a mental list of loosely defined wishes. When I woke up the day after retirement, I felt strange not having to do my morning routine and not knowing exactly what I was supposed to do with myself. So many things I wanted to do after retirement seemed trivial and even unnecessary. There was really nothing left for me to do.

I began blaming myself for my rash decision to retire. I felt that my usefulness to society had suddenly ended. My coworkers had promised me that they would call me for technical support work. No calls had come. A depression started to set in. It was a rough first month. I felt that I had become a parasite to the society, eating the food that should go to those who contributed. I did not think I could go on like that.

Just before I retired, in anticipation of consulting for Duke Energy, I formed my own company, which I named JJK Water Technology Inc. after consulting with many folks, including my daughter. She suggested that I name it I Know Water Inc., which sounded catchy and creative. But I decided against it because it also sounded too lightweight. Forming of my own company was probably one of the best decisions I have ever made. It is in its seventh year, and it has helped us finance our new home on the East Coast. But, most importantly, it has kept me sane. My feeling of uselessness has gradually receded.

Last year, I finally visited my homeland with my wife for the first time. She had been to Korea several times. But financial difficulties had kept me from visiting. At one point, my bad back became an issue; I had a back problem for years. Driving or sitting for too long tended to aggravate it. I did not think my back could endure being strapped in a seat during a ten-hour flight, but I wanted to see my homeland before I die.

As we landed at the Inchon airport, I thought I had landed in the wrong country. My homeland had transformed into an economic powerhouse—a far cry from the impoverished country I had left behind forty-some years before.

My siblings in Korea had arranged for a guided bus tour around the country. I became emotional when I saw them. My older brother looked older. But my two younger sisters looked younger and more beautiful. I had met them all in United States on several occasions, but separately. It was the first time I had seen them all together. My younger brother and his wife traveled from Thailand to join us. He and his wife were doing missionary work, running an orphanage there.

As our bus was heading toward Busan—the second-largest port city in southern Korea—I saw jagged mountains that arose above the horizon in a distance. As our bus drew closer to the city, I saw that they were not mountains but rows of high-rise buildings. The next day, our bus tour took us to Ulsan, where the Hyundai car factories and shipyards were. As our bus climbed over the top of a hill overlooking this port city, I saw that the whole city was engulfed by one gigantic industrial complex.

A few days later, my sister drove me to our old neighborhood, where I spent most of my childhood and adolescence. The whole area was unrecognizable and foreign to me. I knew that forty years was a long time, but I did not think that much change was possible. But I consoled myself by thinking that if changes are inevitable, it's better that they be forward changes rather than regressions.

The primary purpose of my visit was to relive my childhood memories and find my belongingness. But it was clear that there was no home to go to. It seemed that I had relinquished my right to call it home by being absent so long. I thought I had finally reached the end of my journey to find peace with myself. But I had not, and this saddened me deeply.

My daughter visited with our barely three-year-old grandson, Jack, and five-months-old granddaughter, Rosemary, this winter. It was her third visit in three years. Fairbanks was having record cold temperatures. It was nice that they picked the best time. It is strange that of so many cities and towns in the lower 48, she had chosen to live in Fairbanks – the city where I spent my first two memorable years of my life in America. Rosemary was only barely able to sit when she came but had begun to crawl when she left. It was amazing to watch her grow in such a short time. She would be walking when we saw her on her next visit. At three years and one month, Jack was expressing himself so well that it almost scared me.

He would walk up to any stranger, young or old, to chat. One day I took him to a Food Lion to get several grocery items my daughter wanted. As soon as I took him out of the car in the parking area, he was already chatting with a woman and asking her to find him a buggy. She was so amused, as it was probably her first time to be asked such a thing by a little toddler. As he found one in the shopping cart corral, he dashed and lunged himself into the buggy cabin and sat on the driver's seat with his hands on the steering wheel.

Inside the store, as I strolled around. Suddenly, he jumped out of the buggy, grabbed a box of donut holes, put it in his buggy, and rode back. I remembered that his mom had taken him to this store and bought some on her previous trip. My first reaction was to take it from him and put it back, as it was not on her grocery list. But I abandoned that idea, as I did not want to see his face change from excitement to major disappointment.

As expected, Tonia reproached me for getting the donut holes. "You bought it first," I retorted. She told him to have just one after eating good food. As soon as he ate several baby carrots, he demanded the "donut balls."

"Donut holes," I said. He had a puzzled look, and I thought, *Shouldn't those be called donut balls?*

I took two out of the box and placed them on the plate. "One for you and one for me," I said. I left my partially eaten donut hole on the plate while I was reading a book. He'd already finished his and started to grab mine. "That's mine," I declared.

"I am just holding it, "he responded.

"Oh, okay," I said.

The next thing I saw was him holding it in front of his wide-opened mouth. I was incapable of taking it away from him—and a joy along with it. I nodded to him to go on and eat it. His joy was immense. As I was watching him eating, I wondered if children become hostage to the vagaries of grownups, and if we have a right to place so many temptations in front of them.

I enjoyed time with them so much. I cannot remember when I had such a wonderful time with my own children. Come to think of it, I cannot remember any quality time with my wife either. I was so absorbed in my job. I took my family for granted. Now I regret that deeply.

CHAPTER 5-1

Fishing Trip to the Outer Banks, NC

We all gathered at our house the day before the fishing trip. Sue, Sang's wife brought a lot of delicious Korean dishes and fish seasonings. She even brought home-brewed blackberry wine that was simply out of the world. Sehwan and his wife, Chris traveled all the way from Tampa, Florida. I had spent many hours preparing for the trip. I had gone out for quite a few days to catch the mullets off our dock with a cast net. I kept them in the Zip-loc bags and stored them in the freezer. I was told that bait fish would be hard to find and expensive even if we find them over there. I replaced my three fishing poles with 30lb lines and 6oz sinkers in anticipation for hauling in some big fish.

Believe me, when I heard many unbelievable stories from folks, who had been there before, my mouth was drooling, wondering if I would ever have a chance to go there and to experience what they had. Now, we were going. I don't remember when I have been this excited. I read the same excitement on Sehwan's face. He is a true angler. He loves fishing more than anything else.

My four-wheel drive was jam-packed with six of us and our belongings inside and with two coolers in the hitched cargo carrier outside. All three women were squeezed in the second-row seat. Sang crouched down in the third row back seat all by himself during most of our trip. His lower body was literally buried under the suitcases, groceries and fishing gear. I felt bad about it. However, this did not prevent him from butting in every conversation. "I am too fat to be seated there," declared Sehwan. I, of course, was a driver. We drove through the beautiful winding NC coastal roads. Roads cut through marshes along the coastline. It had to be high tide as the water reached the edge of the shoulder on both sides of the road. The ferry ride from Cedar Island to Ocracoke was over 2 hours long. I thought it was a little too long and boring. Sehwan and Chris were enjoying every minute of it, as it was their first ferry ride.

After a short second ferry ride that connects Ocracoke to Cape Hatteras, we finally arrived at our two story, wood framed, rented house. It was not a fancy place by any stretch of imagination, but it had 4 bedrooms, 3 baths and a large family room with a kitchen, which overlooks the ocean.

The next day, we traveled about 10 miles north to Cape Hatteras Lighthouse, where we purchased a permit to drive over the knee-deep sand beach to the fishing destination. It was a one-way narrow path rutted deep by the repeated use of four wheelers on the beach. Several vehicles were stuck in front of us, causing a major traffic jam. At the gate, we were told to deflate the tires to 20lbs to get more traction on sands. *Some folks probably forgot to do it,* I said to myself. We were bitching about the stoppage and feeling smug while waiting for the passage to be cleared. Many got out of their vehicles, including Sang and Sehwan to help push the stuck vehicles. Finally, the passage was cleared. We were moving again. The scene was surreal: I was fantasizing that we were part of pioneers exploring a new frontier on the uncharted East Coast.

Finally, we reached the destination. It is a thumb-shaped spit of land, which juts out into the deep ocean. The beach was already occupied with the vehicles, which lined up along the shore. The waves were high, crashing the shore with roars. *Can't wait to throw the first line,* I murmured to myself in excitement. To catch a big one, I wanted to throw the line farther out there behind where the waves start to form. I dashed out between waves, threw the line and dashed back to the shore. Soon, I realized that I was not in my 40's. I could not outrun the waves. I got wet from head to toe more than a few times. Who said "60 is the new 40?" To make the matter worse, no fish were biting, or there were no fish to bite. I looked around to observe other anglers on the beach. No one was hauling in any fish. The first thing that crossed my mind was why on earth so many folks were out here. It seems that they all came here just like us, wishing to catch a monster fish that they heard or dreamt about. It was disappointing. I let my friends down, or worse yet, I felt that I lied to them. Then, in my defense, someone had lied to me first and I was a mere messenger. We went back to the house frustrated. On the way back, we stopped by several fishing spots on the sound side. Not a single bite.

Early next morning, we, only the three men went back to the same beach, thinking that fishing is better in the morning and we had already paid $50 for a 3-day permit. *We have to catch something to show for our time and effort,* I murmured to myself. The beach was just as crowded as the day before. And the outcome was the same. We had to come home empty-handed.

After dinner, we went to the beach across the street from our rented house. They say that fish bite better in the evening and at night. It was perfect October weather, not too hot, not too cold, with overcast skies. Sehwan was fishing. Sang and I were standing next to him, watching him. Soon, my eyes were wandering, often fixing on half naked women passing by. Chris, Sue and my wife were all on the beach. I spotted a large crowd gathered on the shore, half a mile and so yonder. Sang and I decided to go and investigate. It was a woman they were looking on. She was reeling in something big. Her fishing rod was bending to the point of breaking. She was resting her rod on her thigh with her knees bent. She was pulling the rod towards her with all her strength and then quickly reeling in to gain ground. She was repeating this process for a long time. It was getting dark. All onlookers had left. *Is she trying to tire out the fish?* I murmured to myself. But it seemed that the fish was tiring her out instead. Her husband or more likely her boyfriend, was just standing there, not giving her a helping hand. He was a much younger looking, tall guy. *Maybe, he did not want to take fun away from her. Or is she a cougar?* I thought to myself. Finally, it grew totally dark. Luckily, Sang had a flashlight. He was helping her with his flashlight. I was watching it for well over an hour and the fish was no closer to the shore. It dawned on me that when she pulled her rod up, the line was slipping off the reel, and she was winding the line that had been slipped. This means that she was not making any ground. She could go on all night long without making any headway. I whispered this to Sang, hoping he would come to his senses and leave her. It was so dark. I could not see a person several feet away. Sang was kind of in a quandary, knowing that if he left, this poor woman would not be able to see anything in front of her. I was worried about how long his flashlight would last. It was not even a flashlight, but a mosquito zapper with a flashlight handle. I was wondering what happened to Sehwan. *If he were here, he could put some sense into Sang's head,* I murmured. Sehwan sometimes gets so involved in fishing that he fails to recognize the surroundings. He could have been swept away by rising tides and waves in the dark. Over the roaring sounds of waves, there is no way anyone could hear him yelling for help. Besides, it was pitch dark and all the beachgoers had left the area. Reluctantly, I left to convey this awkward situation to Sehwan, if I could find him. I ran where he had been before, screaming my lungs out, calling his name. I was out of breath, gasping for air. I did not know how far I ran, but my inner voice told me that I had gone too far and need to come back if I have any chance to find him. It was so dark, and I could not see even myself. A thought came to me that this is how a person feels just before he or she dies. I did not know where it came from, but I gained my second wind and was able to double back to where Sang was. He was still shining his flashlight. His flashlight got dimmer and dimmer. Finally, he had come to his senses. He said to her "I am sorry, but we have to go." With that, we left her.

We knew we had to walk along the beach and then cross over the dune towards our house. However, we were not sure how far we had to walk back before making a turn toward the dune. It seemed that all the houses looked alike as we could see only dim lights coming from the houses afar. The night was moonless and overcast. There was not even a single star that could be seen in the sky, not that it could help us. I did not know that a place could be this dark. Sang told me that he recognized the dune, but we could not find the path to access to the other side of the dune. I knew that he often says things, which are not based on the fact, but guided by hunches and gut feelings. But I knew I had to follow him because at least he had a hunch while I did not have anything to go by. As we stumbled over the dune, an unfamiliar landscape appeared in front of us. "We need to go right," said he. "There is no path. I see only thick bushes," I shot back. As I was standing in despair, not knowing what we need to do next, I heard people laughing from a distance. First, I thought that I was hallucinating, hearing something that was not there, but it was real human laughing. I told Sang that we needed to go where the laughing was heard. He was shaking his head and wanted to stick to his original plan – to walk through the bushes. Although I did not want to go a separate way, my instinct told me that I needed to go towards the laughing. It was a hard decision, but I knew I was certain. So, I left him. There were a bunch of people shooting the breeze while watching over chickens on a grill. I asked if anyone knew the street named "Runboat Circle," where our rented house was situated. It surprised me that I was able to recollect the street name. They were not locals but from out-of-state. One fellow said that he could find it out. He, then, was pulling a smartphone or something out of his pocket. It turned out that Runboat Circle is five blocks away. He told me that I should turn left at the end of his driveway, walk a few blocks to Hwy 12, then turn right, walk 5 blocks to reach Runboat Circle. In this part of the island, blocks are not well defined and two adjacent blocks can be far apart. It would be a long walk, for sure, but I knew exactly how to find my way home now. After leaving the folks, I could not find Sang. My first thought was that he had left all by himself. He would be wandering through the tall bushes all night and at some point, his legs would give out or he could trip over some object protruding from the ground. Who knows what after that? I called his name, hoping he had not gone too far. Next thing I knew, he had followed me stealthily all the way and had been hiding behind a parked car on the street, eavesdropping my entire conversation with the party folks. Before I explained what we need to do, he said, "No." This time, he wanted to go back down to the beach and start fresh from there. My reaction was that he had led us to this place in the first place. What makes him think that he would find his way home now? If he knew this area so well, why had he not found our place already? I know now how to find our place even though it is a long walk. I was so sure that he would come to his senses and goes along with my plan. No, he insisted on his gut feeling. When I glanced at his face, he had that grim look. I knew then that he was not about to change his mind. I thought that he had lost his mind due to the ordeal we had just gone through, remembering that I had almost lost mine when I could not find Sehwan at the beach. When you are not yourself, this kind of illogical thinking occupies the afflicted mind. This is how people end up dying. Reluctantly, I agreed to go with him. I did not want to walk alone in the dark for such a long walk.

So, we went over the dune and back down to the beach again. One thing we learned, after I met those party folks, was that we still needed to go several blocks farther. This helped us greatly. As we approached the bottom of the dune, out of nowhere, a lightning flashed across the sky, and then an ear-piercing bang. The next thing I saw was Sang taking off, saying gibberish. I said to myself, *where can he go? Certainly, lightning can outrun him many thousand times faster.* It is not a bear running after us. When a bear is after us, all you have to do is to outrun the other guy, but it is lightning. The bear logic would not hold here.

Now, I could see some objects on the beach close to the dune as some of streetlights cast dim light over the beach. Finally, as I caught up with him, he was saying that he now recognized the beach umbrella left standing on the sands. Come to think of it, I too remember seeing something like that on the way out to beach.

Thank heaven, we finally made it to our rented house. As I was nearing the house, I was thinking to myself, *we need to call 911 and ask the operator to send for a search team to the beach. It would look bad to our ladies, particularly to Chris, that we came home alone without her husband.* As I approached the house, I heard Sehwan laughing loudly from inside the house. Wow, I was so relieved that he was home safe. But then, I was upset that I had wasted my time or worse yet, risked my life looking for him. Upon entering the house, I confronted him and asked angrily, "Why did you come home without us?" "You had told me that you would be back but had not returned. So, I thought you had gone home," he said. "Well, for all the more reason, you should have been looking for us. And, if someone said to you that he would be back but has not come back, would that not bother you?" I retorted. He said, "I am sorry." It was hard to argue further when he said that, although I knew he utters these words all the time without compunction, just to avoid conflicts. Soon, Sang and I got into a major verbal brawl. I enumerated all the events in a chronological order and accused Sang of his errors in judgment, which almost cost my life. Sue and Chris were laughing their hearts out. My wife had retired early to her room. I felt smug, knowing these two ladies were on my side. No sooner had I finished than Sang began his version of story to dispute my account of the events. These two ladies were laughing just as hard. It was amazing how he was able to twist and spin the facts to his benefit. But to his credit, he was just as convincing as I was, at least to the ladies.

We decided to return to my house two days earlier than the scheduled check-out date. More fishing was out of question and there was not much else to do besides fishing. I called the rental office and asked the lady to refund our unused two-day rent. She said she was not authorized to do that. Then, I spoke with the manager and explained why we need to leave early. "This place has no internet connections and we need to check on something for our business," said I. Of course, I had to stretch the truth a little. We argued for a while. In the end, "We are sorry, but you can come to our office to check on your internet," he replied. I knew all along that they would not refund the unused time, but I thought it wouldn't hurt to ask. We got back to our home without much fanfare. After dinner, we were on our pier, hoping to catch some fish to make up for the unsuccessful fishing expedition. The water was unusually high, almost reaching the top of the dock. It was a dark, breezy and moonless night. I don't remember if I ever came out here this late for fishing. However, Sehwan was not about to let that bother him. He ordered me to bring a flood light to plug in the outlet on the dock. To our surprise, fish were biting. We caught two large black drums, one large black sea bass and several croakers. *We should have been fishing here all along rather than going to the Outer Banks,* lamented Sehwan. The next day, we fished again at about the same time. Absolutely, no bites I tried to come up with some plausible or cockamamie theory, but I could not think of any. Sang and Sue had left earlier as they had business to attend to. Sehwan and Chris were to leave the following day early in the morning as they had to travel for good 10 hours. He was at it again. He caught several good-sized croakers and two lizardfish. He was using shrimp and cut-up pin fish as bait. At my suggestion, he switched to the live mullets, which I had caught with my cast-net. Before long, lo and behold, he was dragging something big. As he pulled it up, the head of a flounder began to emerge out of water, then, it wiggled off the hook into the water and swam away. I told him that he needed to use a net to scoop it up instead of pulling it out of water. He nodded his head to indicate that he got the message and wanted me to stop lecturing him.

Based on my past encounters with flounder, they are not a fighter like drum are in the water. But they don't like to be out of water. Duh, what fish does? Besides, they have a small mouth relative to their body. Mullet are sometime too big for a flounder to swallow whole. This makes it difficult to raise the flounder out of water as a mullet in its mouth just breaks loose. Surprisingly enough, a short time later, he caught another flounder. I could see its whole body in water. I was ready to help him this time with a net. Much to my dismay, he was pulling it up again. Of course, it got away. I chastised him for his carelessness. "I was trying to bring it close to the surface to find out what I've got," he responded in a rather unsure voice. I felt sorry for what sounded like I was raising my voice at him. I often get myself in hot water as my wife does not appreciate my raised voice.

Next morning, Chris and Sehwan were out in the garage, preparing for trip back home. As Sehwan opened the tailgate of his car, I saw a huge cooler occupying the entire width of back space. He had to carry back this cooler with no fish in it. I felt a lump rising in my throat. I let him down. Then, I remember a quote from Ralph Emerson: *Life is a journey, not a destination.* It seems to fit our trip well. I had fun along the way. Hope they did too.

CHAPTER 6

Aging

Life has gone by so fast. When I look in the mirror, I see an old man. And I wonder how I got this old.

As I get older, it seems that I can't help looking back and reliving my past. Would I have done differently if I could start all over again? Have I achieved my dreams? I've found answers to these questions elusive. I was relieved to know that my perception of my past with my children is far different from that of my children. During my daughter's last visit, I confessed to her that I had been so involved with my work that I had neglected spending much time with her and her brother. I was surprised to hear her say that she had a wonderful childhood and that Mom and I did a good job. She thanked me for that. It meant so much to me. I realized that I have good memories of my childhood during the Korean War, though I am certain my parents would not have thought I would.

Looking back, I do not have many regrets, but have many what-ifs. If I have one regret, it is that my children don't speak to each other. In fact, it has been that way since they were pretty young. I regret that I have not done more to bring them closer to each other. What could I have done differently? I am still grappling with this lingering unanswered question. Were their personalities so incompatible? Was it because she favored Asian students less than their white counterparts, including her own brother? Maybe it was Paul who thought it was that way. It saddens me to think that after I die, they will become strangers to each other.

I have lived for almost all my adult life here in the United States, yet I am lonely at heart. The country that has given me so much, yet it has taken so much away from me. I want to go home where I feel I truly belong. I know it is a fantasy—not a dream. What if I had not come to America? What if I had gone back to Korea earlier? What if I had left the United States before I met my wife? What if...? I know these are all moot points, yet I marvel at how much my life could have been different. "Could her life have been happier and more fulfilling?" I wonder. Could mine?